CONTENTS

INTRODUCTION

In today's tech and finance scene, Bitcoin has caught a lot of attention and raised many questions. This book is here to help you understand Bitcoin without the fuss. Each section stands on its own, tackling different aspects of Bitcoin, from its environmental impact to how it operates. You can jump to any section that interests you without having to go through it in order, making learning about Bitcoin flexible and straightforward.

This guide is designed to make Bitcoin accessible to everyone, regardless of your background. It's a place where you can find clear answers to your questions, presented in a way that's easy to understand. Think of this book as a helpful friend guiding you as you learn more about Bitcoin, at your own speed and depth.

The aim here is to offer a resource that's both easy to understand and useful, helping to turn your curiosity into knowledge. Whether you're just starting out or looking to deepen your understanding, this book is here to assist you in exploring the world of Bitcoin.

Join the conversation at bitcoinbuddy.co to learn more and connect with a community ready to explore the world of Bitcoin with you.

21 QUESTIONS ABOUT BITCOIN

Bitcoin is complicated. There are no dumb questions.

BITCOIN BUDDY

WHAT IS BITCOIN?

In today's digital era, we're witnessing the rise of a new kind of currency that's changing the financial scene: Bitcoin. This term has been buzzing around, sparking interest and a bit of confusion. Let's explore the realm of Bitcoin step by step, avoiding the complex terminology. Essentially, Bitcoin is a digital currency, a virtual asset that exists solely online. It made its debut in 2009, introduced by the mysterious entity or group named Satoshi Nakamoto. It differs from the usual currencies like dollars or euros, which are controlled and issued by governments, as Bitcoin functions on a decentralized network. This means it isn't linked to any government or institution. It's a user-driven project that distributes power among its community, encouraging a spirit of equality and independence.

You might be curious about how this digital currency remains secure and structured without a central authority supervising it. This is where the innovative blockchain technology steps in. Imagine a digital ledger, a highly secure online record book that diligently logs all Bitcoin transactions. This ledger isn't confined to a single place or governed by one organization. Instead, it's dispersed across a massive network of computers worldwide, establishing a strong and transparent system where data, once entered, is permanent and unchangeable.

To expand this digital record, a procedure called mining occurs. Mining resembles a sort of competition where individuals, referred to as miners, vie to be the first to confirm and safeguard a batch of transactions, or in simpler terms, to add a new block to the chain. This competition isn't based on luck but on computational prowess. Miners utilize potent computers to compete, and the first to finish the task is rewarded with new bitcoins, injecting new units into the market. This method guarantees the safety and seamless functioning of the Bitcoin network.

Now, let's discuss how one can integrate Bitcoin into daily life. To begin using Bitcoin, you first need a digital wallet, a software where you can keep, transfer, and receive bitcoins. It's your personal entry point to the digital currency world, somewhat akin to how an email program allows you to send and receive emails. Once you've set up a wallet, you can obtain bitcoins either by purchasing them on an exchange with conventional money or by accepting them as payment for goods or services. Utilizing Bitcoin is quite simple, particularly if you're accustomed to online banking or mobile payment apps. Transactions are peer-to-peer, happening directly between users without a middleman, like a bank. This direct approach not only speeds up transactions but also lowers the fees involved. It's a contemporary, digital method of exchanging cash, but with global accessibility and heightened security.

Regarding its value, it's vital to mention that Bitcoin's worth can be highly unstable. Its value can swing dramatically in a short time, attracting traders and investors eager to capitalize on these fluctuations. However, this volatility also implies that it can be a somewhat precarious investment, not suitable for everyone. Bitcoin has evolved into a worldwide sensation, breaking through borders and offering a universal medium of exchange accessible to people globally. Its decentralized aspect means it isn't influenced by the economic strategies of any single government, making it a genuinely international currency. This feature has found favor in areas with fluctuating currencies or stringent economic policies.

To sum up, Bitcoin signifies a notable change in how we view and utilize money. Its decentralized, transparent, and secure attributes present a new angle on financial transactions, returning power to individual users. As we traverse this digital era, it's thrilling to contemplate the potential influences and advancements Bitcoin might ignite in the financial sector and beyond. It's more than a currency; it's a step towards a more inclusive and democratic financial system. So, as you delve into the Bitcoin world, remember to proceed with caution, recognizing that, like any financial endeavor, it carries its unique set of risks and opportunities.

WHO CREATED BITCOIN?

In the late 2000s, as the world was grappling with the financial crisis, a remarkable invention quietly emerged in the digital realm. The creation of Bitcoin, a new kind of money, promised a future where financial transactions could be more transparent, secure, and decentralized. The mastermind behind this revolutionary concept was an individual or a group of individuals known as Satoshi Nakamoto.

The true identity of Satoshi Nakamoto remains one of the most intriguing mysteries of the digital age. Despite being the creator of one of the most disruptive technologies in the 21st century, Nakamoto managed to keep their identity a secret. What we do know is that Nakamoto introduced Bitcoin to the world through a whitepaper titled "Bitcoin: A Peer-to-Peer Electronic Cash System" published in 2008. This document laid the groundwork for what would become the world's first cryptocurrency.

In the whitepaper, Nakamoto outlined the fundamental principles that govern Bitcoin. They envisioned a financial system where transactions could occur directly between parties without the need for a central authority, like a bank or government. This vision was grounded in a deep understanding of both economics and cryptography, the science of secure communication.

Nakamoto was actively involved in the development and promotion of Bitcoin in its early days. They communicated with other enthusiasts and developers through online forums and email correspondence, guiding the nascent community and refining the Bitcoin software. Despite their active involvement, Nakamoto was always careful to maintain their anonymity, communicating solely through digital channels and never revealing any personal details.

In 2009, Nakamoto mined the first block of the Bitcoin blockchain, also known as the Genesis Block or Block 0. This event marked the birth of the Bitcoin network, a system that operates on a decentralized network of computers. Nakamoto continued to work on the project, collaborating with other developers and making improvements to the system.

As Bitcoin began to grow and attract a larger community of users and developers, Nakamoto gradually reduced their involvement. In 2011, they handed over control of the source code repository and network alert key to a software developer named Gavin Andresen, a prominent figure in the Bitcoin community. Around the same time, Nakamoto also transferred several domains associated with Bitcoin to various prominent members of the community. This transition marked the end of Nakamoto's visible involvement with the project, and they faded into the background, leaving the stewardship of Bitcoin to a growing community of developers and enthusiasts.

Despite their departure, the principles Nakamoto instilled in Bitcoin continue to guide its development. The decentralized nature of the network, where no single entity has control, and the transparent and immutable record of transactions on the blockchain, remain central to Bitcoin's identity.

The creation of Bitcoin was not just the introduction of a new currency. It was a radical rethinking of how financial systems could operate, with an emphasis on decentralization and peer-to-peer transactions. It challenged the traditional notions of trust and authority in financial transactions, proposing a system where trust is established through cryptographic proof rather than through central institutions.

The legacy of Satoshi Nakamoto, therefore, extends beyond the creation of Bitcoin. They sparked a movement that has grown into a vibrant community of people who believe in the potential of decentralized financial systems. Moreover, Nakamoto's invention paved the way for the development of a myriad of other cryptocurrencies and blockchain projects, each building upon the foundational principles laid out in the Bitcoin whitepaper.

Today, as we witness the continued growth and evolution of the cryptocurrency space, the identity of Satoshi Nakamoto remains elusive. Various theories and claims regarding Nakamoto's identity have surfaced over the years, but none have been substantiated. In many ways, the anonymity of Bitcoin's creator has become a powerful symbol of the decentralized ethos that underpins the cryptocurrency movement. It serves as a reminder that in the world of Bitcoin, the focus is not on individuals but on the collective effort to build more open, transparent, and decentralized financial systems.

In the grand scheme of things, perhaps it doesn't matter who Satoshi Nakamoto is. What matters is the innovation they brought to life and the waves of change it has set in motion in the financial world. Bitcoin stands as a testament to human ingenuity and the potential for transformative change when technology is leveraged to create more open and inclusive financial systems.

HOW DOES
BITCOIN WORK?

Understanding how Bitcoin works can initially seem a bit daunting, especially if you're new to the world of digital currencies. But fret not, we're here to break it down into digestible pieces that will hopefully make the whole concept a lot clearer. Let's dive right in!

At its core, Bitcoin operates on a decentralized network, which means it isn't governed by any central authority or institution. This decentralized nature allows for a level of transparency and security that is quite unique in the financial world. Now, let's explore some of the key components that make the Bitcoin network tick.

First and foremost, we have the blockchain, a public ledger that records all transactions made with Bitcoin. This ledger is maintained by a network of computers, also known as nodes. These nodes validate and record transactions on the blockchain, ensuring that all transactions are legitimate and preventing double-spending. The blockchain is essentially a chain of blocks, where each block contains a list of transactions. This chain grows over time as new blocks are added, creating a comprehensive and immutable record of all transactions that have ever occurred on the network.

Now, let's talk about mining, which is a crucial process in the Bitcoin network. Mining is somewhat like a lottery where miners compete to add new blocks to the blockchain. Miners use powerful computers to verify transactions by finding a specific number, which is a solution to a complex mathematical problem. The first miner to find the correct number gets to add a new block to the blockchain and is rewarded with newly minted bitcoins and transaction fees. This process not only facilitates transactions but also secures the network and introduces new bitcoins into circulation.

To engage in transactions, you'll need a digital wallet, which is a software application where you can store, send, and receive bitcoins. Each wallet has a private key, known only to the owner, and a public address, which is like an email address that others can see. When you send bitcoins, you are essentially signing off ownership of the coins to the recipient's wallet address. The transaction is then verified by miners and recorded on the blockchain.

The value of Bitcoin is determined by various factors including supply and demand dynamics, market sentiment, and macroeconomic indicators. It's known for its price volatility, which means the value can fluctuate significantly over a short period. This volatility can be a double-edged sword, presenting opportunities for high returns, but also significant losses.

One of the remarkable aspects of Bitcoin is its finite supply. There will only ever be 21 million bitcoins in existence, a feature that was hardcoded into the protocol by its mysterious creator, Satoshi Nakamoto. This limited supply creates a scarcity effect, which is one of the factors that can influence its price.

Using Bitcoin as a means of exchange is relatively straightforward. Transactions are peer-to-peer, meaning they occur directly between users without the need for an intermediary, like a bank. This direct transfer can make transactions quicker and potentially reduce the fees associated with them.

In conclusion, Bitcoin represents a revolutionary shift in the financial landscape, offering a decentralized and transparent alternative to traditional fiat currencies. Its underlying technology, the blockchain, and the mining process ensure the security and integrity of the network, making it an exciting frontier in the world of finance and beyond. As you delve deeper into the world of Bitcoin, you'll discover its potential to reshape the way we think about and use money in a globalized world.

IS BITCOIN REAL MONEY?

Absolutely, **Bitcoin** can be considered real money, but it operates quite differently from the traditional currencies you might be accustomed to. Let's delve into the nuances to help you understand this better.

First and foremost, it's vital to understand that the concept of "real" when it comes to money has evolved significantly over time. In the earliest days of commerce, we traded goods directly, a system known as barter. However, as societies grew more complex, so did the needs of trade, leading to the creation of money as a medium of exchange. Initially, money took the form of physical commodities with intrinsic value, such as gold or silver. Over time, we transitioned to fiat currencies, which are the paper notes and coins issued by governments that we use today. These currencies hold value because the government maintains them and people have faith in their value.

Now, enter **Bitcoin**, a digital currency that represents a new evolution in our concept of money. It exists solely in the digital realm, and its value is not backed by a physical commodity or a government. Instead, its worth stems from a combination of scarcity (there's a limited supply of bitcoins), utility, and the level of demand among users.

Bitcoin operates on a decentralized network, meaning it isn't controlled by any single entity or government. This decentralization is made possible through a technology called **blockchain**, a kind of digital ledger that records all transactions made with Bitcoin. This ledger is maintained by a network of computers, and it's transparent and immutable, which means once a transaction is recorded, it cannot be altered or deleted.

Now, you might be wondering how new bitcoins come into existence. This is where **mining** comes into play. Mining is a process where individuals or groups use powerful computers to validate and secure transactions on the network. You can think of this process as a kind of lottery where miners compete to solve a complex puzzle, and the winner gets rewarded with new bitcoins. This not only introduces new bitcoins into the system but also secures the network and verifies all transactions.

Using **Bitcoin** is akin to using other forms of money, with a few notable differences. To use Bitcoin, you'll need a digital wallet, a tool that allows you to store, send, and receive bitcoins. Transactions are peer-to-peer, meaning they occur directly between users without an intermediary, like a bank. This system can make transactions quicker and potentially cheaper, as it removes the need for a middleman.

When it comes to spending your bitcoins, more and more businesses are starting to accept Bitcoin as a form of payment for goods and services. Moreover, many people view Bitcoin as an investment, holding onto their bitcoins in the hope that their value will increase over time.

However, it's important to note that Bitcoin's value can be highly volatile, experiencing significant fluctuations within short periods. This volatility can present opportunities for traders and investors, but it also brings a level of risk.

So, to circle back to your original question: Is **Bitcoin** real money? Yes, it is a form of money, but it represents a shift in how we perceive and use money, offering a decentralized, digital alternative to traditional fiat currencies. It's a fascinating evolution, illustrating how our concept of "money" is continually evolving to meet the changing needs and complexities of our global society.

WHAT IS A BITCOIN WALLET?

A **bitcoin wallet** is essentially your personal interface to the Bitcoin network, akin to how your online bank account is an interface to the traditional monetary system. It's a digital tool that allows you to store, send, and receive bitcoins securely. Now, let's delve deeper into its intricacies and functionalities.

In the physical world, a wallet is a small, foldable case where you keep your cash, cards, and other small personal items. A bitcoin wallet serves a similar purpose; it's a digital storage solution where you keep your bitcoins. But instead of storing physical currency, it stores the digital credentials necessary to access your bitcoins on the Bitcoin network. These credentials are your private key, a unique digital signature that verifies your ownership of the bitcoins stored in a particular address on the blockchain.

The **blockchain** is a public ledger that records all transactions made with bitcoins. Each transaction is verified and added to the blockchain through a process called **mining**, which is somewhat like a lottery where miners compete to add new transactions to the blockchain. The winner of this lottery gets rewarded with new bitcoins, which is how new bitcoins are introduced into the system. Your wallet interacts with this blockchain to enable transactions.

Now, let's talk about the different types of bitcoin wallets available. There are mainly four types: **software wallets**, **hardware wallets**, **mobile wallets**, and **web wallets**.

Software wallets are applications that you download and install on your computer. These wallets offer a high level of security as they allow you to create a private key that never leaves your device. However, they require some maintenance and backups to prevent loss of bitcoins in case of computer failures.

Hardware wallets are physical devices that store your private keys offline. These wallets are immune to online hacking attempts because the private keys are stored offline. They are considered one of the safest options for storing a significant amount of bitcoins as they are immune to online hacking attempts and malware.

Mobile wallets are smartphone applications that allow you to manage your bitcoins right from your mobile device. These wallets are handy for making transactions on the go, such as paying for goods and services at physical stores that accept bitcoins.

Web wallets are accessible through web browsers and are hosted on online servers. These wallets are convenient for quick access and transactions, but they store your private keys online, making them more vulnerable to hacking attempts and phishing scams.

Regardless of the type of wallet you choose, it's crucial to keep your private keys secure and confidential. Sharing your private keys with others is akin to handing over the keys to your home; it gives others complete access to your bitcoins.

Using a bitcoin wallet is relatively straightforward. To receive bitcoins, you provide the sender with your wallet's public address, a unique identifier linked to your wallet. This public address is like your email address, which you share with others to receive emails.

To send bitcoins, you would enter the recipient's public address and the amount you want to send. The transaction is then verified and recorded on the blockchain.

In conclusion, a bitcoin wallet is an essential tool for interacting with the Bitcoin network. It allows you to store, send, and receive bitcoins securely. Understanding how to use a bitcoin wallet effectively and safely can enhance your experience in the world of digital currencies. Remember, the security of your wallet depends largely on your practices and precautions. Always keep your private keys confidential and use reputable wallets to protect your bitcoins from unauthorized access and potential loss.

HOW DO I SET UP A BITCOIN WALLET?

Setting up a **Bitcoin wallet** is your first step into the world of digital currencies. A Bitcoin wallet functions similarly to a digital bank account, allowing you to send, receive, and manage your bitcoins. Here, we'll walk you through the process of setting up a Bitcoin wallet, step by step, in a manner that's easy to understand, even if you're not a tech-savvy individual.

First, you'll need to choose a **wallet provider**. There are many providers available, offering various types of wallets including web wallets, mobile wallets, and hardware wallets. **Web wallets** are accessible through your web browser, **mobile wallets** are apps downloaded onto your smartphone, and **hardware wallets** are physical devices that store your bitcoins offline for extra security.

Once you've chosen a wallet provider, head to their website or download their app to create an account. This process usually involves providing an email address and creating a password. It's crucial to choose a strong, unique password to ensure the security of your wallet.

After setting up your account, the wallet provider will generate a **Bitcoin address** for you. This address is a string of numbers and letters, and it functions similarly to a bank account number. You'll use this address to receive bitcoins from others. It's a public address, meaning others can see it, but they can only use it to send bitcoins to you, not withdraw them.

Next, you'll encounter something called a **private key**. This is a secret series of numbers and letters that allows you to access and manage the bitcoins in your wallet. It's vital to keep your private key confidential, as anyone who has access to it can control your bitcoins. Most wallet providers will help you secure your private key, often encrypting it to add an extra layer of security.

At this point, you might be wondering how to get bitcoins into your new wallet. One way is to purchase bitcoins from a **Bitcoin exchange**. These are platforms where you can buy bitcoins using traditional currencies, like dollars or euros. Once you've bought bitcoins, you can transfer them to your wallet using your Bitcoin address.

Another way to acquire bitcoins is through **mining**, which is a kind of lottery where participants use powerful computers to compete to validate transactions on the Bitcoin network. The winner of this lottery is rewarded with new bitcoins. However, mining is a complex and resource-intensive process, so it might not be the best method for beginners to acquire bitcoins.

Sending bitcoins from your wallet is a straightforward process. You'll need the Bitcoin address of the person or entity you want to send bitcoins to. Simply enter this address and the amount of bitcoins you want to send in the appropriate fields in your wallet, and click "send". It's as simple as that!

Receiving bitcoins is just as easy. Provide your Bitcoin address to the person or entity sending you bitcoins. They will enter this address in their wallet to send bitcoins to you. You can find your Bitcoin address in your wallet, usually in a section labeled "receive".

Remember, all transactions made with Bitcoin are irreversible.

Once you've sent bitcoins, you cannot get them back unless the recipient agrees to send them back to you. Therefore, always double-check the details of your transactions before you click "send".

In conclusion, setting up a Bitcoin wallet is a simple and straightforward process. By following these steps, you'll be well on your way to participating in the exciting world of Bitcoin. Remember to keep your private key secure and to use your wallet responsibly.

HOW DO I SEND AND RECEIVE BITCOIN?

To begin your journey with **Bitcoin**, it's essential to understand how to send and receive this digital currency. It might seem a bit daunting at first, but once you get the hang of it, you'll find it's as easy as sending an email or a message through your favorite app.

First things first, you'll need a **digital wallet**. This is a virtual wallet where you can store your bitcoins. There are various types of wallets available, including mobile wallets, web wallets, and hardware wallets. Depending on your preference and the level of security you desire, you can choose the one that suits you best.

Once you have your wallet set up, you'll be given a **Bitcoin address**, which is akin to having an email address. This address is a string of letters and numbers, and it's what people will use to send bitcoins to you. Similarly, if you want to send bitcoins to someone, you'll need their Bitcoin address.

Now, let's say you want to send bitcoins to a friend. You would open your wallet, select the option to send bitcoins, and then enter your friend's Bitcoin address and the amount you want to send. It's always a good practice to double-check the address to avoid any errors, as transactions on the Bitcoin network are irreversible. Once everything looks good, you can proceed to send the bitcoins.

On the other hand, if you are on the receiving end, the process is even simpler. All you need to do is share your Bitcoin address with the person who wants to send you bitcoins. They will follow the process mentioned above, and once they send the bitcoins, you will see them in your wallet. It might take a few minutes for the transaction to be confirmed by the network, but don't worry, it's a normal part of the process.

Now, you might be wondering how these transactions are verified and recorded. This is where **mining** comes into play. Mining is a kind of lottery where individuals or groups, known as miners, compete to validate transactions on the network. The first one to validate a block of transactions gets rewarded with new bitcoins and transaction fees. This process not only helps in validating and securing transactions but also introduces new bitcoins into the system.

Security is a significant aspect of Bitcoin transactions. The Bitcoin network operates on a technology called **blockchain**, which is a public ledger containing all transactions ever made with Bitcoin. This technology ensures that once a transaction is recorded, it cannot be altered or deleted, providing a high level of security and transparency.

While using Bitcoin, you'll also encounter terms like **private keys** and **public keys**. Your private key is like a digital signature, a secret code that proves your ownership of the bitcoins in your wallet. It's crucial to keep this key secure and never share it with anyone. The public key, on the other hand, is derived from the private key and is used to create your Bitcoin address. It's a bit like your phone number, something you can share with others without compromising your security.

As you become more comfortable with the process of sending and receiving bitcoins, you might also explore additional features and settings in your wallet, such as adding a description to your transaction or setting transaction fees. These features can enhance your experience and provide more control over your transactions.

In conclusion, sending and receiving bitcoins is a straightforward process that involves using a digital wallet and a Bitcoin address. With a focus on security and transparency, the Bitcoin network offers a robust platform for peer-to-peer transactions, free from the control of centralized institutions.

WHAT IS A BITCOIN ADDRESS?

A **bitcoin address** is a unique identifier that allows you to receive bitcoins. Think of it as a kind of digital postbox where others can send you bitcoins. Each address is a string of alphanumeric characters, which might seem a bit complex at first glance, but this complexity ensures the security and privacy of your transactions.

To get a bit more technical but still keeping it simple, a bitcoin address is generated from a cryptographic hash of a public key. When you create a wallet to store your bitcoins, a private key and a public key are generated. The private key is like the key to your home; it's meant to be kept secret and secure, as it allows you to access and spend the bitcoins stored at a particular address. The public key, on the other hand, is used to create your bitcoin address, and it's what others will use to send bitcoins to you.

Now, let's talk about how you can get a bitcoin address. When you set up a **bitcoin wallet**, which is a digital tool that allows you to manage your bitcoins, it will automatically generate a bitcoin address for you. You can create multiple addresses within the same wallet, which can be handy for organizing your transactions or maintaining privacy.

When someone wants to send you bitcoins, you provide them

with one of your bitcoin addresses. It's a one-way street – they can only send bitcoins to the address, but they can't access or view the bitcoins you have there. This is a crucial aspect of the security and privacy features inherent in the bitcoin network.

Now, you might be wondering how transactions work in the bitcoin network. When someone sends bitcoins to your address, the transaction is recorded on the **blockchain**, a public ledger that contains the details of all bitcoin transactions that have ever occurred. This blockchain is maintained by a network of nodes, which are computers participating in the bitcoin network.

The process of confirming transactions and recording them on the blockchain involves a kind of lottery called **mining**. In this lottery, miners compete to confirm a block of transactions and add it to the blockchain. It's not a lottery in the traditional sense, but rather a process where miners use computational power to be the first to confirm a block of transactions. The winner of this lottery is rewarded with new bitcoins, which is how new bitcoins are introduced into the circulation. This process is integral to maintaining the security and integrity of the bitcoin network.

Using a bitcoin address is quite straightforward. When you want to receive bitcoins, you simply share your bitcoin address with the sender. And when you want to send bitcoins, you would need the recipient's bitcoin address. It's a simple process of giving and taking, facilitated by unique identifiers that help in maintaining a secure and efficient network.

In essence, a bitcoin address is your identity on the bitcoin network, allowing you to receive bitcoins in a secure and private manner. It's a critical component in the functioning of the decentralized, peer-to-peer bitcoin network, facilitating secure and transparent transactions that are recorded on a public ledger, accessible by anyone and everyone. It's a revolutionary system that combines the benefits of modern technology with the principles of financial autonomy and privacy.

Remember, while your bitcoin address is public, your private key should remain confidential to ensure the security of your assets. It's akin to the relationship between an email address and its password. Sharing your email address is fine, but sharing the password compromises your security. Similarly, while it's okay to share your bitcoin address, keeping your private key secure is of utmost importance.

In conclusion, a bitcoin address is more than just a string of letters and numbers. It's your gateway to the world of bitcoin, a unique identifier that allows you to participate in a global financial network, where transactions are secure, transparent, and not controlled by any central authority. It's a small yet significant part of a larger movement towards a more open and decentralized financial system.

WHAT IS THE BLOCKCHAIN?

Imagine a bustling city where every transaction, big or small, is recorded meticulously in a giant, immutable ledger. This ledger isn't stored in a single place or controlled by a single entity; instead, it's distributed across a network of computers, each holding a copy of this extensive record. This, in essence, is the **blockchain**, a technology that underpins Bitcoin and other cryptocurrencies.

At its core, the blockchain is a digital ledger that records all transactions made with a particular cryptocurrency. It's a transparent and secure way of tracking and verifying all exchanges, ensuring that every transaction is legitimate and preventing fraud and double-spending. Let's delve deeper into the fascinating world of blockchain to understand its nuances and why it's considered revolutionary.

The blockchain is made up of a series of blocks, each holding a list of transactions. These blocks are linked together in a chronological chain, forming a cohesive and unbroken record of all transactions that have ever occurred on the network. Each block contains a unique code, known as a **hash**, which is generated based on the information it holds. This hash is a bit like a digital fingerprint, uniquely representing the block's contents.

Now, let's talk about how new blocks are added to this chain. This process is where the concept of **mining** comes into play. Mining is akin to a kind of lottery where miners compete to add the next block to the chain. Miners collect a bunch of transactions, verify them, and then compete to find a specific hash that meets certain criteria. The first miner to find this hash gets to add the block to the chain and is rewarded with newly minted bitcoins and transaction fees. This process not only helps in adding new blocks to the blockchain but also secures the network and ensures the integrity of the data.

One of the standout features of the blockchain is its **decentralized nature**. Unlike traditional systems where a single entity, like a bank or government, has control, the blockchain operates on a network of computers, also known as nodes. Each node has a copy of the entire blockchain, and they work together to maintain and update the ledger. This decentralization means that no single entity has complete control over the entire blockchain, making it more secure and resistant to fraud and manipulation.

Another remarkable aspect of the blockchain is its **transparency**. Since the ledger is open and accessible to anyone, it fosters a level of transparency that is not seen in many other financial systems. Anyone can view the transactions on the blockchain, and once a transaction is added, it cannot be altered or deleted. This immutability is a significant deterrent to fraud and corruption, as it creates a permanent and unchangeable record of all transactions.

Using blockchain technology, Bitcoin has introduced a new way of conducting transactions that is open, transparent, and secure. It eliminates the need for intermediaries, allowing for peer-to-peer transactions that are quick and inexpensive. Moreover, it offers a level of security and transparency that is often lacking in traditional financial systems.

As we explore the intricacies of how to use Bitcoin, understanding the blockchain's workings is fundamental. It's not just a technological backbone for cryptocurrencies but a revolutionary system that has the potential to change the way we think about and handle financial transactions. Its applications are vast, and its potential is still being realized, with many industries exploring ways to integrate blockchain technology to enhance transparency, security, and efficiency.

In conclusion, the blockchain is a groundbreaking technology that underpins cryptocurrencies like Bitcoin. Its decentralized, transparent, and immutable nature offers a fresh perspective on financial transactions, paving the way for a more open and secure financial future. As you venture deeper into the world of Bitcoin, a solid understanding of the blockchain will serve as a vital foundation, helping you navigate this new frontier with confidence and knowledge.

ARE BITCOIN TRANSACTIONS REVERSIBLE?

Bitcoin transactions, once confirmed, are not reversible. This is a fundamental characteristic that sets it apart from traditional financial systems where transactions can sometimes be reversed, especially in cases of error or fraud. This irreversible nature of Bitcoin transactions is deeply rooted in the principles of blockchain technology, which is the underlying technology that powers Bitcoin.

When you initiate a Bitcoin transaction, it first goes into a pool of unconfirmed transactions. Miners then pick up these transactions to include them in a new block. The process of creating a new block is somewhat like a lottery, where miners compete to find the solution to a complex problem. The first one to find the solution gets to add the new block to the blockchain, and the transactions included in that block are considered confirmed. This process typically takes about 10 minutes, but it can vary.

Once a transaction is confirmed and added to the blockchain, it becomes a permanent part of the ledger. This means that it cannot be altered or removed. This permanency is ensured by the cryptographic hashes that link each block to the previous one, creating a secure and unbreakable chain. If someone were to attempt to alter a transaction, it would change the hash of the block, breaking the link with the previous block and alerting the network to the discrepancy.

The irreversible nature of Bitcoin transactions brings both benefits and challenges. On the one hand, it prevents fraud and double-spending, which is a scenario where someone tries to use the same bitcoin for more than one transaction. It also means that transactions are transparent and verifiable by anyone on the network, fostering trust and security within the system.

On the other hand, the irreversible nature of transactions means that if you make an error, such as sending bitcoins to the wrong address, there is no way to retrieve them. Similarly, if someone gains unauthorized access to your Bitcoin wallet and transfers your bitcoins, there is no mechanism to reverse the transaction and recover the lost funds. This places a significant responsibility on the users to ensure the security of their private keys, which are the cryptographic keys that allow access to their bitcoins.

To mitigate the risk of irreversible errors, it is essential to double-check the details of your transactions before confirming them. Many wallet applications also provide features like address book and confirmation prompts to help prevent errors. It's also crucial to maintain the security of your wallet by using strong passwords and keeping backup copies of your private keys in secure locations.

Furthermore, to protect yourself from unauthorized access and potential loss, you might consider using a hardware wallet, which is a physical device that stores your private keys offline, making it immune to online hacking attempts. You should also be cautious of phishing scams and other fraudulent activities that aim to steal your private keys.

In conclusion, while the irreversible nature of Bitcoin

transactions can be seen as a strength, offering transparency and security, it also comes with a set of responsibilities for the users. It emphasizes the importance of being cautious and diligent when conducting transactions, ensuring the security of your assets, and understanding the workings of the system to use it effectively and safely.

WHAT ARE TRANSACTION FEES?

Transaction fees are a vital part of the Bitcoin network. When you send bitcoins to someone, you are essentially broadcasting your transaction to a network of computers, known as nodes. These nodes validate and record transactions on the blockchain. However, this process isn't done for free; it requires computational power and energy. To compensate for this, a transaction fee is levied on each transaction.

Now, let's delve deeper into why transaction fees are necessary and how they function within the Bitcoin network.

When you initiate a Bitcoin transaction, it joins a pool of other transactions waiting to be confirmed. Miners, who are participants in the network with high-powered computers, pick transactions from this pool to include in a new block of the blockchain. But here's the catch: a block can only contain a limited amount of data, which means only a finite number of transactions can be included in each block.

This is where the transaction fees play a significant role. Since miners are the ones who validate and secure transactions on the network, they naturally prefer to include transactions with higher fees. It's a bit like a bidding war where transactions compete for a spot in the next block, and miners are more inclined to choose transactions that offer a higher reward. This reward comes from the transaction fees.

Understanding **mining** as a kind of lottery can help you grasp why transaction fees are a crucial incentive for miners. In this lottery, miners compete to find a specific number, and the first one to find it gets to add a new block to the blockchain. The winner of this lottery receives newly minted bitcoins as a reward, along with the accumulated transaction fees from all the transactions included in that block. This dual reward system not only incentivizes miners to participate in the network but also ensures that transactions are validated swiftly.

Transaction fees are not fixed; they fluctuate based on several factors including the demand for block space and the complexity of the transaction. If the network is busy and many people are trying to send transactions at the same time, fees can increase. Conversely, if the network is less congested, fees might be lower.

When you initiate a transaction, you have the option to choose the fee you are willing to pay. Wallets often provide guidelines or automatic settings to help users set appropriate fees. If you opt for a higher fee, your transaction is likely to be processed faster. On the other hand, if you choose a lower fee, you might have to wait a bit longer for your transaction to be confirmed, especially during busy times.

It's also worth noting that transaction fees serve as a security measure for the network. By requiring a fee for every transaction, the network protects itself against spam transactions and potential attacks that aim to overwhelm the network with a large volume of tiny transactions, a scenario that could slow down or halt the network's operation.

In conclusion, transaction fees are an integral component of the Bitcoin network, facilitating the smooth and secure functioning of the decentralized ledger system. They incentivize miners to validate transactions, help prioritize transaction confirmation times, and safeguard the network against potential spam and attacks.

WHY IS BITCOIN VALUABLE?

Bitcoin, often hailed as the pioneer in the world of cryptocurrencies, has carved out a significant place in the financial sphere, and many people find themselves asking, "Why is Bitcoin valuable?" To answer this question, we need to delve into various facets that contribute to its value: its scarcity, decentralized nature, security features, and its role as a pioneer in the cryptocurrency space.

At its core, **Bitcoin** is a digital asset that operates on a technology called **blockchain**. This technology ensures that all transactions are recorded in a secure and transparent manner. The blockchain is like a digital ledger that is immutable, meaning once a transaction is recorded, it cannot be altered or deleted. This feature instills a high level of trust and security in the system, making Bitcoin a reliable medium for transactions.

One of the most significant factors contributing to Bitcoin's value is its **scarcity**. Just like precious metals like gold, Bitcoin has a limited supply. There will only ever be 21 million bitcoins in existence. This scarcity is built into the code of Bitcoin itself, a feature that mimics the scarcity of precious metals. This limited supply creates a sense of value, as people often attribute worth to rare items.

The process of bringing new bitcoins into circulation is known as **mining**, which can be likened to a kind of lottery. In this lottery, miners compete to validate transactions on the network. The winner, or the one who validates the block of transactions, is rewarded with new bitcoins. This process not only secures the network but also ensures the gradual release of new bitcoins into the system, controlling the influx of new coins and thereby helping maintain its value.

Another vital aspect that adds to Bitcoin's value is its **decentralized nature**. Unlike traditional currencies, which are controlled by central banks or governments, Bitcoin operates on a decentralized network of computers. This means that no single entity has control over the currency, making it immune to government interference or manipulation. This decentralization offers a kind of financial freedom, where your assets are truly your own, without the risk of seizure or devaluation by any central authority.

Furthermore, Bitcoin offers a level of **divisibility** that is not seen in other forms of assets. A single bitcoin can be divided into 100 million smaller units called satoshis. This divisibility allows for micro-transactions and makes Bitcoin adaptable to various levels of value, adding to its utility and, by extension, its value.

Bitcoin's role as a **pioneer** in the cryptocurrency space cannot be understated. Being the first of its kind, it has established itself as a well-recognized and trusted brand in the financial market. Its pioneering status has given it a head start in adoption and development, creating a network effect that adds to its value. The more people use and accept Bitcoin, the more its value is likely to increase.

Moreover, Bitcoin has opened up a world of possibilities in the financial sector, offering a **global and inclusive financial system**.

It can be sent or received by anyone, anywhere in the world, without the need for intermediaries. This global reach not only adds to its utility but also contributes to its value, as it can serve as a universal medium of exchange, uniting people from different parts of the world in a new financial ecosystem.

In conclusion, the value of Bitcoin is derived from a combination of its scarcity, security features, decentralized nature, and its pioneering role in the cryptocurrency space. Its ability to offer a transparent, secure, and inclusive financial system has positioned it as a valuable asset in the modern world.

WHAT DETERMINES THE PRICE OF BITCOIN?

Understanding what determines the price of Bitcoin can sometimes feel like unraveling a big, intricate puzzle. At its core, the price of Bitcoin is influenced by a variety of factors, ranging from basic principles of supply and demand to the broader economic landscape. Let's delve into these factors one by one to get a clearer picture.

First and foremost, **supply and demand** play a pivotal role in determining the price of Bitcoin. Just like any other commodity, if more people want to buy Bitcoin than sell it, the price goes up, and vice versa. This is a fundamental economic principle that governs the pricing of many things, from apples in a grocery store to stocks on the stock market.

Market sentiment is another significant factor. This refers to the collective attitude of investors towards Bitcoin at any given time. Various elements can influence market sentiment, including news reports, government regulations, technological developments, and broader economic trends. For instance, if a prominent business leader endorses Bitcoin, it might stir positive sentiment, potentially driving up the price. Conversely, negative news reports or regulatory crackdowns can foster negative sentiment, possibly leading to a decrease in price.

Now, let's talk about **mining**, which is akin to a kind of lottery. In this process, miners compete to add new blocks to the blockchain by being the first to validate a group of transactions. The winner of this lottery is rewarded with new bitcoins. This not only introduces new coins into the system but also influences the supply, and consequently, the price of Bitcoin. As more bitcoins are mined, the reward decreases, and the overall supply grows more scarce, which can potentially drive up the price.

Market manipulation is an unfortunate reality in the world of cryptocurrencies. Sometimes, individuals or groups with significant resources can manipulate the price of Bitcoin to their advantage. This could be through spreading false information to stir sentiment or by making large trades to create artificial demand or supply. It's always good to be aware that such manipulations can occur, and to approach investments with a critical eye.

The **utility and adoption** of Bitcoin also influence its price. As more businesses start accepting Bitcoin as a form of payment, and as more people use it for various transactions, its utility increases. This, in turn, can have a positive effect on the price. Moreover, developments that enhance the functionality and usability of the Bitcoin network can also make it more attractive to users, potentially driving up demand and price.

Lastly, **macroeconomic factors** can have a bearing on the price of Bitcoin. For instance, inflation, changes in interest rates, and economic crises can influence investor behavior. In some cases, people turn to Bitcoin as a hedge against economic instability, which can increase demand and, subsequently, the price.

In conclusion, the price of Bitcoin is determined by a complex interplay of various factors, including supply and demand dynamics, market sentiment, the process of mining, potential market manipulation, utility and adoption levels, and broader macroeconomic factors.

HOW DO I BUY BITCOIN?

Buying **Bitcoin** can often seem like a daunting task, especially if you're new to the world of digital currencies. But fret not, it's not as complex as it might initially seem. Let's break it down step by step.

First and foremost, you'll need a **digital wallet** to store your bitcoins. A digital wallet is a kind of virtual bank account that allows you to send or receive bitcoins. There are various types of wallets available, including mobile wallets, web wallets, and hardware wallets. Depending on your preference for security and convenience, you can choose one that suits you best.

Once you have your wallet set up, the next step is to find a **Bitcoin exchange**. These are platforms where you can buy bitcoins using traditional currencies like dollars or euros. It's essential to choose a reputable exchange to ensure the safety of your transactions. You would need to create an account on the chosen platform, providing some personal information and verifying your identity, much like opening a new bank account.

Now, you're ready to buy your first bitcoins. On the exchange, you'll find various buying options, which might include bank transfers, credit card payments, or even other digital currencies. Choose a payment method that you're comfortable with and enter the amount of Bitcoin you wish to purchase. It's worth noting that you don't have to buy a whole bitcoin; you can buy a fraction of a bitcoin to start with, which might be a more approachable option if you're just getting started.

After deciding on the amount and payment method, you proceed to make the purchase. Once the transaction is completed, the bitcoins will be transferred to your wallet. It's a good practice to transfer your bitcoins from the exchange to your personal wallet to ensure their safety, as exchanges can sometimes be prone to hacks or other security issues.

Now, let's talk a bit about **mining**, as it's another way to acquire bitcoins, albeit a more complex one. Mining is a kind of lottery where individuals or groups compete to validate transactions on the Bitcoin network. This process involves using powerful computers to verify transactions on the network. The first one to validate a block of transactions wins a reward in the form of new bitcoins and transaction fees. It's a competitive and resource-intensive process, and nowadays, it's mostly undertaken by people with specialized equipment.

Buying bitcoins is just the beginning of your journey into the world of digital currencies. As you become more familiar with the process, you might explore other aspects of the Bitcoin ecosystem, like trading or using bitcoins to make purchases online. Remember, the world of Bitcoin is ever-evolving, and there's always something new to learn.

In conclusion, buying Bitcoin is a straightforward process that involves setting up a digital wallet, choosing a reputable Bitcoin exchange, and making a purchase using traditional currency. Whether you decide to hold onto your bitcoins as an investment or use them to make online transactions, you're now part of a global community that is reshaping the way we think about money and financial transactions.

CAN I BUY LESS THAN ONE BITCOIN?

Absolutely, you can buy less than one bitcoin. In fact, one of the beautiful aspects of Bitcoin is its divisibility, which allows you to own a fraction of it. This fraction of a bitcoin is called a **satoshi**, named after the pseudonymous creator, Satoshi Nakamoto. One bitcoin is equivalent to 100 million satoshis, making it possible to own a very small portion of a bitcoin.

Now, you might be wondering why you'd want to buy less than one bitcoin. The reason is quite simple: a single bitcoin can be quite expensive, with its value fluctuating greatly over short periods. Buying a fraction of a bitcoin allows you to invest or transact with a smaller amount of money, making the cryptocurrency accessible to more people.

When you decide to buy a fraction of a bitcoin, you'll be using a **digital wallet** to store your cryptocurrency. This wallet functions similarly to a bank account, but it's for storing and managing your bitcoins. You can think of it as a personal interface to the Bitcoin network, just like your online bank account is an interface to the traditional monetary system.

Buying less than one bitcoin is a straightforward process. You'll first need to choose a **cryptocurrency exchange** to facilitate your purchase. These exchanges are platforms that allow you to buy, sell, and hold cryptocurrencies. Once you've set up an account on an exchange, you can specify the amount of bitcoin you want to buy, down to the satoshi. This means you can spend as little or as much money as you'd like to acquire bitcoin.

Now, let's talk a bit about how new bitcoins come into existence, which happens through a process called **mining**. Mining is akin to a kind of lottery where participants, called miners, compete to add new blocks to the blockchain, which is a public ledger containing all bitcoin transactions. Miners use powerful computers to validate transactions and secure the network. The first miner to complete this task gets to add a new block to the blockchain and is rewarded with new bitcoins and transaction fees. This process not only introduces new bitcoins into the system but also secures the network and verifies all transactions.

Using bitcoin, whether a whole one or just a fraction, is a peer-to-peer process. This means that transactions occur directly between users without an intermediary, like a bank. This direct transfer can make transactions quicker and potentially reduce the fees associated with them. It's a bit like handing over cash to someone, but in a digital space, with the assurance that the transaction is secure and transparent.

The value of bitcoin, whether you own a whole one or just a fraction, can fluctuate widely within a short period. This characteristic has made it a subject of interest for traders and investors looking to profit from price swings. However, this volatility also means that it can be a somewhat risky investment, and it might not be suitable for everyone.

Bitcoin has transcended borders, offering a universal means of exchange that can be used by people all over the world. Its decentralized nature means that it is not subject to the economic policies of any single government, making it a truly global currency. This characteristic has made it particularly appealing in regions with unstable currencies or restrictive economic policies.

In conclusion, buying less than one bitcoin is not only possible but also a common practice, especially for those who are new to the world of cryptocurrency or those who prefer to invest smaller amounts. It's a great way to familiarize yourself with the process of buying, storing, and using bitcoin without committing a large amount of money.

WHAT IS A BITCOIN MINER?

A **bitcoin miner** is an individual or a group of individuals participating in the Bitcoin network to validate and secure transactions. This process is crucial in maintaining the decentralized nature of the system, ensuring that transactions are legitimate and helping to prevent fraud and double-spending.

To understand the role of a bitcoin miner, it's essential to first grasp the concept of the **blockchain**, which is the underlying technology of Bitcoin. The blockchain is a public ledger that records all transactions made with Bitcoin. This ledger is decentralized, meaning it is distributed across a network of computers globally. Each transaction made is added to a block, and several such blocks form a chain, hence the term blockchain. This chain of blocks is visible to everyone within the network, promoting transparency and security.

Now, let's delve deeper into the role of a bitcoin miner in this ecosystem. Miners use powerful computers to validate transactions on the network. This validation process is akin to a kind of lottery. Miners compete to find a specific number, and the first one to find it gets to add a new block of transactions to the blockchain. This isn't just a game of luck; it requires substantial computational power and energy resources. The "winning" miner, or the one who successfully adds a new block to the blockchain, is rewarded with newly minted bitcoins and transaction fees from the transactions included in the block. This is how new bitcoins are introduced into the circulation, and it's also how miners make a profit from their efforts.

The process of mining, therefore, serves two primary purposes: it validates and secures transactions, and it generates new bitcoins. It's a critical process that maintains the integrity and functionality of the Bitcoin network.

Using Bitcoin involves making transactions with a digital currency called bitcoins. When someone makes a transaction, it is broadcast to the network and placed in a pool of unconfirmed transactions. Miners select transactions from this pool to validate and include in a new block. Once a block is filled with transactions, miners engage in the lottery-like process to compete to add this block to the blockchain. This process involves finding a specific number through trial and error, which requires substantial computational power.

The role of a bitcoin miner can be likened to that of a security guard who keeps an eye on all transactions happening in a vast marketplace. They ensure that all transactions are legitimate and secure, maintaining the trust and functionality of the system. The lottery-like process they engage in is a mechanism that not only rewards them for their efforts but also ensures the decentralized nature of the system, preventing any single entity from having control over the network.

In the early days of Bitcoin, mining could be done using regular personal computers, and later, graphics cards. However, as more people joined the network and the difficulty of the lottery process increased, the computational power required to mine bitcoins increased substantially. Today, mining is a highly specialized activity, with miners using sophisticated machines, including ASIC (Application-Specific Integrated Circuit) devices, which are specifically built for the purpose of mining bitcoins.

Mining is not just a process of making a profit through earning new bitcoins. It is a fundamental aspect of the Bitcoin network that maintains its decentralized, secure, and transparent nature. It's a symbiotic relationship where miners are incentivized to participate in the network, and their participation, in turn, ensures the network's security and functionality.

WHAT IS PROOF OF WORK?

Proof of work is a fundamental concept in the world of Bitcoin and other cryptocurrencies. It's a method used to ensure the security and integrity of transactions on a decentralized network. Let's delve into this concept in a way that's easy to grasp.

Imagine a group of miners, not with pickaxes and helmets, but equipped with powerful computers, all participating in a kind of lottery. This isn't a lottery with tickets bought at a store, but rather a competition to validate and secure transactions on the Bitcoin network. The "ticket" to this lottery is the solution to a complex computational problem, which requires substantial computational power and energy to solve.

The first miner to find the solution gets to add a new block of transactions to the blockchain, the digital ledger that records all Bitcoin transactions. This new block then undergoes verification by other nodes or computers in the network, a process that ensures the validity of the transactions contained within it. Once verified, the block is added to the chain, and the winning miner is rewarded with newly minted bitcoins and transaction fees. This entire process is what we refer to as proof of work.

Now, you might wonder why it's called "proof of work". The name comes from the fact that the network can easily verify or "prove" that a miner has done the "work" necessary to find the solution to the computational problem. This work, in essence, serves as a testament to the miner's efforts and the computational power expended during the process. It's a way to discourage malicious activities and to ensure that adding new blocks to the blockchain requires a significant amount of work, making it secure and tamper-resistant.

Proof of work is not just a security measure but also a consensus mechanism. In a decentralized network like Bitcoin, where there is no central authority to validate transactions, it's crucial to have a system in place that ensures everyone agrees on the state of the blockchain. By requiring miners to do work - to compete in the lottery - to add new blocks, proof of work ensures that all participants in the network agree on the validity of transactions and the order in which they occur. It's a democratic process, where the consensus is achieved through computational effort, not through a central authority's decree.

However, it's worth noting that proof of work has its critics. The process requires a significant amount of energy, as miners around the world use powerful computers that consume a lot of electricity to compete in the lottery. This has raised environmental concerns, leading some to explore alternative consensus mechanisms that are less energy-intensive, such as proof of stake, where the creator of a new block is chosen based on their ownership or stake in the cryptocurrency.

Furthermore, proof of work can lead to a concentration of power in the hands of a few miners who have the resources to operate large mining farms with significant computational power. This has raised concerns about the decentralized nature of cryptocurrencies, as it could potentially lead to a centralization of control in the hands of a few powerful miners.

Despite these criticisms, proof of work has proven to be a robust and secure consensus mechanism, successfully underpinning the Bitcoin network since its inception in 2009. It has played a crucial role in the growth and development of cryptocurrencies, providing a secure and decentralized way to validate transactions and achieve consensus in a network where trust is not established through central authorities but through computational work and effort.

In conclusion, proof of work is a cornerstone in the world of cryptocurrencies, a mechanism that ensures security, integrity, and consensus in a decentralized network. It's a fascinating concept that combines elements of cryptography, computer science, and economic incentives to create a secure and decentralized financial system.

DO I HAVE TO PAY
TAXES ON BITCOIN?

Absolutely, discussing taxes is a crucial part of understanding the financial responsibilities that come with using or investing in Bitcoin.

When you engage in transactions using Bitcoin, whether it's buying goods or services, or trading it as an investment, you might incur tax obligations. The exact details can vary greatly depending on your jurisdiction, as different countries have their own rules and regulations regarding the taxation of cryptocurrencies.

In many places, Bitcoin is considered a form of property, which means that you might be required to pay capital gains tax when you sell it at a profit. **Capital gains tax** is a tax on the profit realized on the sale of a non-inventory asset. The most common capital gains are realized from the sale of stocks, bonds, precious metals, real estate, and property. In the context of Bitcoin, this would mean that if you bought Bitcoin at one price and then sold it at a higher price, the difference (or "gain") could be taxable.

Now, let's say you are paid in Bitcoin for a service or product you provided. This transaction is considered a form of income, and you would need to report it as such. You would calculate the amount of income based on the value of Bitcoin at the time you received it.

Moreover, if you are a miner who earns Bitcoin through the mining process, this also could be considered a form of income. Remember, mining is akin to participating in a kind of lottery where you might be rewarded with new bitcoins for verifying and recording transactions on the blockchain. This reward, too, might be considered taxable income.

It's also important to note that charitable donations made in Bitcoin might be deductible, depending on your local tax laws. This means that if you donate Bitcoin to a recognized charitable organization, you might be able to deduct the value of the donation on your tax return.

Given the complexity of tax laws and the relatively new and evolving nature of cryptocurrency regulations, it's highly recommended to consult with a tax professional who has experience with cryptocurrencies. They can provide guidance tailored to your specific situation and help ensure that you comply with all necessary tax obligations.

In summary, yes, you might have to pay taxes on Bitcoin transactions, and these can come in various forms including capital gains tax and income tax. It's essential to keep detailed records of your Bitcoin transactions to assist in accurate reporting at tax time. Remember, being informed and proactive about your tax obligations can help you avoid potential pitfalls and penalties in the future.

CAN BITCOIN BE BANNED?

In the world of finance and technology, Bitcoin has emerged as a revolutionary force, challenging the traditional notions of currency and transactions. One of the pressing questions that many people have is whether Bitcoin can be banned. To address this, we need to delve into the decentralized nature of Bitcoin and the implications of attempting to impose restrictions on it.

Bitcoin operates on a decentralized network, which means it isn't controlled by any single entity or government. This network is maintained by a group of people known as miners who validate transactions through a process akin to a lottery. In this lottery, miners compete to validate transactions recorded on the blockchain, a transparent and immutable digital ledger. The winner of this lottery is rewarded with new bitcoins, a process that not only facilitates transactions but also generates new units of the currency.

The decentralized structure of Bitcoin makes it inherently resistant to censorship or bans. Since there isn't a central authority that governs Bitcoin, shutting it down would be a complex endeavor. Governments can impose restrictions on the exchanges where bitcoins are traded for traditional currencies, making it more challenging for people to buy or sell bitcoins. They might also restrict or ban businesses and service providers from accepting Bitcoin as a payment method.

However, banning Bitcoin entirely is a different ball game. It would mean shutting down a global, decentralized network, which is practically impossible. Even if one country imposes stringent restrictions or bans Bitcoin, the network can still operate seamlessly in other parts of the world. The peer-to-peer nature of Bitcoin transactions allows individuals to send and receive bitcoins without requiring approval from a central authority, making it exceedingly difficult to impose a complete ban.

Moreover, the open-source nature of Bitcoin's software means that the code is available to anyone who wants to use, modify, or distribute it. This accessibility fosters a resilient and adaptable ecosystem. In the event of regulatory crackdowns, it's conceivable that the community could create forks or variations of Bitcoin to circumvent new restrictions, much like how the internet has adapted to various forms of censorship over the years.

While the technical aspects of banning Bitcoin present significant hurdles, there are also legal and economic considerations to take into account. In democratic societies, imposing a ban on Bitcoin might be seen as an infringement on individuals' rights to freely use and transact in the currency of their choice. Moreover, Bitcoin has become a substantial economic force, with many investors, businesses, and financial institutions having vested interests in its growth and stability.

That said, the regulatory landscape surrounding Bitcoin is still evolving. Governments around the world are grappling with how to approach this new form of currency, and their stances vary widely. Some countries have embraced Bitcoin, seeing it as an opportunity to foster innovation and economic growth. Others have imposed restrictions to various degrees, citing concerns about potential misuse, economic stability, and consumer protection.

In conclusion, while governments can certainly impose restrictions that might hinder the use and adoption of Bitcoin, completely banning it poses significant technical, legal, and economic challenges. The decentralized, open-source, and global nature of Bitcoin makes it a resilient system, capable of adapting to changing regulatory environments.

WHAT IS A BITCOIN HALVING?

In the world of Bitcoin, the term **halving** refers to the reduction of rewards that miners receive for verifying and recording transactions on the blockchain. Before we delve deeper into the concept of halving, let's first understand the role miners play in the Bitcoin network.

Miners are individuals or groups who use powerful computers to validate transactions on the Bitcoin network. This process is akin to a kind of lottery where miners compete to be the first to validate a new block of transactions. The winner of this lottery is rewarded with new bitcoins, which are generated with each new block. This reward is essentially how new bitcoins are created, a process that infuses new units of the currency into the market.

Now, when Bitcoin was first created, the reward for mining a block was 50 bitcoins. However, Satoshi Nakamoto, the pseudonymous creator of Bitcoin, designed the system so that this reward would be halved approximately every four years. This event is what we refer to as a **bitcoin halving**. The purpose of this halving is to gradually reduce the number of bitcoins entering circulation, a mechanism that mimics the scarcity and gradual depletion of precious metals like gold.

As time goes on, the reward for mining new blocks decreases, which in turn reduces the rate at which new bitcoins are created. This process will continue until the maximum supply of 21 million bitcoins is reached, a limit that is hardcoded into the Bitcoin protocol. Once this limit is reached, miners will no longer receive block rewards, but will instead be compensated through transaction fees, which are small fees users pay to have their transactions included in a block.

The concept of halving is crucial in maintaining the economic model of Bitcoin. It creates a sort of deflationary effect, as the decreasing supply of new bitcoins entering the market exerts upward pressure on the price, assuming demand remains constant or increases. This is in stark contrast to fiat currencies, which can be printed in unlimited quantities by central banks, often leading to inflation.

Halving events are significant moments in the life cycle of Bitcoin, often accompanied by speculative interest and media attention. Many in the community view these events as milestones that mark the transition to different phases in the maturity of the digital asset. It's a time of anticipation, as market participants speculate on how the halving will influence the price and the overall dynamics of the Bitcoin network.

Understanding the halving process gives insight into the scarcity-driven economic model of Bitcoin, a model that aims to offer a hedge against the inflationary tendencies of traditional fiat currencies. It's a glimpse into the carefully thought-out mechanics that govern the supply of Bitcoin, a digital asset that combines the scarcity properties of precious metals with the transferability and divisibility of digital currencies.

WILL BITCOIN DESTROY THE ENVIRONMENT?

The conversation surrounding **Bitcoin** and its environmental impact has been a hot topic of discussion, with various viewpoints on its potential effects on our planet. To delve into this, we first need to understand the process of **Bitcoin mining**, which is often at the center of these environmental concerns.

Bitcoin mining is akin to participating in a kind of lottery where miners compete to validate transactions on the network. This process requires a significant amount of computational power, and consequently, energy. The energy consumption of the Bitcoin network has raised concerns because it often involves the use of fossil fuels, which contribute to carbon emissions and climate change.

However, it's essential to note that the narrative surrounding Bitcoin's environmental impact is not entirely negative. In fact, the Bitcoin network has been found to drive innovations in the energy sector, including the utilization of **stranded energy** resources. Stranded energy is energy that is wasted as it cannot be economically transported or used. Bitcoin mining can harness this otherwise wasted energy, turning a potential environmental liability into an asset.

Moreover, the Bitcoin network has been instrumental in promoting **methane mitigation**. Methane, a potent greenhouse gas, is often released into the atmosphere during oil extraction processes. Innovative projects have emerged where Bitcoin mining operations are powered by methane that would have otherwise been vented into the atmosphere, thus reducing its environmental impact.

Furthermore, the Bitcoin industry has been a significant player in incentivizing **renewable energy production**. The decentralized nature of the network means that mining operations can be set up in locations with abundant renewable energy resources, such as hydroelectric or solar power. This can potentially lead to an increase in investments in renewable energy projects, fostering a greener energy sector.

It's also worth mentioning that the traditional financial sector and many other industries have substantial environmental footprints. In comparison, the Bitcoin network strives to be more transparent about its energy consumption, providing an opportunity for ongoing improvements and innovations in environmental sustainability.

As we navigate this conversation, it's vital to approach it with a nuanced perspective, acknowledging both the challenges and the opportunities presented by Bitcoin in the environmental sphere. While the concerns about its energy consumption are valid, the potential for Bitcoin to drive positive change in the energy sector and contribute to environmental conservation efforts is significant.

In conclusion, whether Bitcoin will "destroy" the environment is a complex question with no straightforward answer. It presents both challenges and opportunities, and its ultimate impact on the environment will depend on how its potential to foster innovations in the energy sector is leveraged.

ABOUT THE AUTHOR

Joel Klabo

 Joel is the creator of Bitcoin Buddy whos goal is to educate as many people as possible about the benefits of Bitcoin. Bitcoin is complicated, there are no dumb questions.

Check out bitcoinbuddy.co to keep learning and connect with others.